FINGERS COME IN FIVES

29

OLIVER G. SELFRIDGE

Drawings by

MURRAY TINKELMAN

1966

Houghton Mifflin Company
Boston

5 5 5 5 5 5

A NUMBER is an answer to "how many?" Everybody uses numbers, but some people are a little afraid of them. This small book tells some well-known things about numbers, and also some not so well-known things. There is almost no arithmetic.

A good way to start is to ask how old you are, or how many letters there are in your name, or how many brothers and sisters you have, and see what it says here about that number. It is also possible just to start at the beginning, which is Number One.

There are lots of small numbers here, and they are all interesting. There are, of course, many big numbers that are interesting too, but I have put in just a few of my own favorites. I hope the ones that I left out will not feel hurt because of it. They are my friends, all of them, and I hope they can be yours too.

1

1

ONE

One is an easy number and a hard number. Every number is made up of Ones. Very many things are the One and only things like themselves in the whole world.

For instance, there is only One of you, and there is only One of me.

It is easy to follow your nose because you have just One. (Where would you put another? Alongside?)

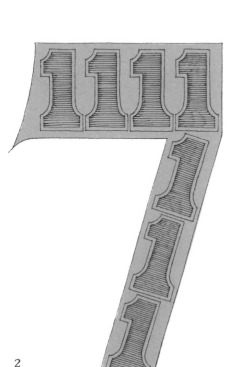

An elephant also has just One trunk.

A plant called bloodroot grows just One leaf and One flower every year. It is very shy and usually lives in deep shade in the forest.

A unicycle has just One wheel, and it is much the hardest kind of cycle to learn to ride, because there are so many different ways to fall off.

There is a saying that One bad apple sours the barrel because the badness can rub off and make the others rotten too. That means that you cannot say that something is perfect if it has One mistake.

The ace, or One, in a deck of cards, is strange because it is sometimes not as strong as a Two and sometimes stronger than all the others.

A talk given by just One person alone is called a monologue or soliloquy, and not a conversation, which takes any number more than One.

Maine is the only state in the United States that touches just One other state.

United States Route One is a road that runs from the most Eastern point of Maine down to the bottom of Florida. It is sometimes called the Post Road, because the mail used to go on it.

The United States is One country. That is what the "united" means.

Two is you and me.

Shoes come in Twos — that's because feet do.

Another kind of Two is a Pair. Shoes come in Pairs. Scissors and trousers also come in Pairs. Practice saying, "I have a Couple of parents," which means the same thing. You do not have permission to say, "I have a Brace of parents." A Brace of pistols is Two pistols, but only pistols, dogs, and dead birds come in Braces. I don't know why.

If you are walking a tightrope, you have Two ways to go, forward and backward. I hope that's enough for you!

With Two faucets you can make your bath as hot or as cold as you like. Otherwise you have to take it the way it comes. And to steer a car, there are Two directions to turn the steering wheel, left and right.

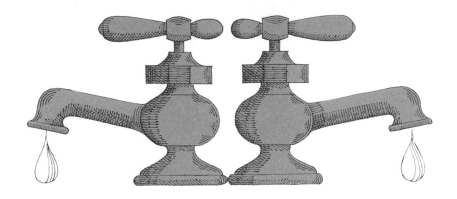

Tandem also means Two, one behind the other; like Two people on a Tandem bicycle, which also has its wheels in Tandem.

Enormously many things come in Pairs, or Couples, or Twos, which makes it easy to find names if you happen to have two pets — like dogs or iguanas. Gog and Magog are Two giants that lived in England a long time ago. Rome was founded before that by Romulus and Remus, who were Twins. When a mother has Two children at the same time they are called Twins; but Twins can be any Two things that look and act alike. Tweedledum and Tweedledee are Twins. A Twin-engined airplane has Two engines. Minneapolis and St. Paul are the Twin cities in Minnesota.

When it is raining hard, people say that it

is raining cats and dogs. You can make up your own phrases with Two ingredients.

Try: It is snowing mooses and meathooks.

Or: The sun is shining jelly and jam.

Of course, opposites come in Twos. Black and white, east and west, winter and summer, go and come, work and play, questions and answers, and so on. Many words have opposites one way or another, but not all of them. What's the opposite of a table?

If you don't have a choice of at least Two things, you don't have any choice at all.

A Duet is a performance by Two people of a piece of music. A Duel is a fight between Two people. One of them challenges the other, and the one who is challenged has the right to choose the weapons, like swords or pistols. Duels are illegal in this country.

3
THREE

Traffic lights usually come in Threes — red and yellow and green. In New York there are only red and green. Poor New York.

Triplets are not so common as twins, but when they come, they come in Threes.

Three is the right number of legs for a tool. If it has fewer than Three, it will fall down. If it has more than Three, it can wobble, unless all the legs are just exactly the right length.

They say that troubles come in Threes, like poison ivy leaves. But the leaves of beans and peas also come in Threes, like ordinary clover. Clover with more than Three leaves is hard to find, but not impossible.

A famous dinosaur, Triceratops, had Three large horns on its head. That is what its name means.

A coconut has Three soft spots in the end so that you can make holes to get the coconut milk out of it.

Leash is a special word which means Three for dead birds. "I shot a leash of pheasant" means that we have Three pheasants to eat for supper. Very strange.

There are Three drones on a bagpipe. A drone is a pipe that always plays the same note and only stops when the air gives out. There is another pipe with holes in it so that the piper can play a tune.

There were Three blind mice in the nursery rhyme, and they ran around till they had their tails cut off with a carving knife. I have not been able to find out what it really means, if anything.

The French flag, the *tricolore,* means Three colors, which come in vertical stripes of blue, white, and red.

Three is the smallest number of straight fences that can be put around some piece of land.

FOUR

A room has Four walls; a rug has Four edges. Lots of things come in Fours.

There are Four seasons: winter, spring, summer, and fall, and Four tastes that you can taste in your mouth: bitter, sweet, sour, and salt. The other tastes are mostly smelled with your nose, which is why having a cold makes food taste less interesting.

Dogs and hogs and crocodiles have Four legs. In fact, most large animals have Four legs.

Directions come in Fours: North, South, West, and East.

The flowers of the dogwood tree have Four petals. So do the flowers of a tiny woodland plant called the bunchberry, which also has just Four leaves.

If you stand in the middle of a crossroads, there are exactly Four ways to go.

Four is an unlucky number in Japan. I don't know why.

There are Four letters in the word FOUR. Four is the only number with its own number of letters.

Dragonflies have Four wings.

Violins have Four strings.

If an object has all its sides flat it must have at least Four sides. Cut a piece off a corner of a block and the piece will have Four flat sides.

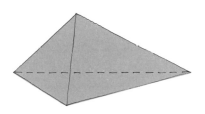

A Square has Four corners, and Four edges which fit in between.

Ancient people used to think that everything was made up of Four things in different amounts. The Four things were Earth, Air, Fire, and Water. If a man was too angry all the time, he had too much Fire in him. If a baby drooled all the time, I suppose he had too much water.

A hand is exactly Four inches, when it is used for telling how high a horse is; you measure the horse to the shoulder, just in front of where you sit, and not to the top of its head.

There are Four precious stones: diamonds, emeralds, rubies, and sapphires.

Forks usually have Four tines. Have you ever heard of a Threek?

5
FIVE

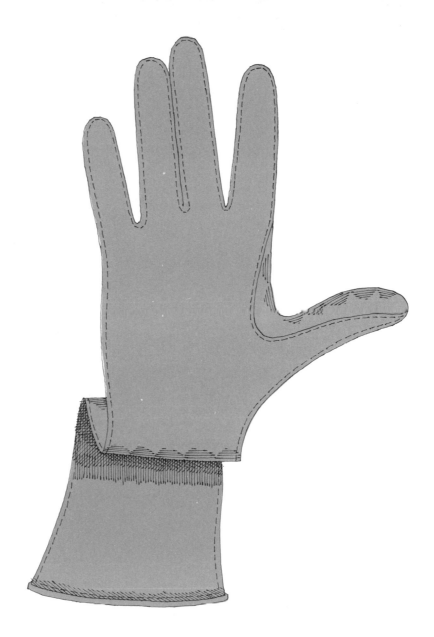

Your feet each have Five toes. Five fingers fit on each hand (just right for gloves!).

Buttercups and apple blossoms have Five petals. If you cut a banana across the middle you will see that it has Five sides, like sand dollars at the beach.

And like starfishes, which usually have Five legs. They are like the stars in our flag which have Five points.

Cut an apple the wrong way, and you will find that kind of star.

When I change a flat tire on my car, there are Five nuts on the wheel, and Five bolts to fit them on.

There are Five Great Lakes: Superior, Michigan, Huron, Erie, and Ontario.

And there are Five great oceans of the world: Atlantic, Pacific, Indian, Arctic, and Antarctic.

Five is the largest number of vowels that occur together in one word in English.*

There are said to be Five senses: seeing,

* The only two words I know with Five vowels together are "miaoued" and "queueing."

hearing, touching, tasting, and smelling. Actually there are lots of others; for example, feeling a headache is not one of those Five; neither is feeling too warm on a hot summer's day.

A nickel is worth Five pennies.

Five-in-a-row is a pleasant and easy game between two people in which you try to place your men in a row of Five, either up-and-down, across, or diagonally on a large board. Once you have placed your men you never move them. In Japan the game is called Go-Moku. It is much more interesting than tick-tack-toe.

There is an extremely large building in Washington where the people work who run the Army, Navy, and Air Force. It has Five sides, which makes it a Pentagon.

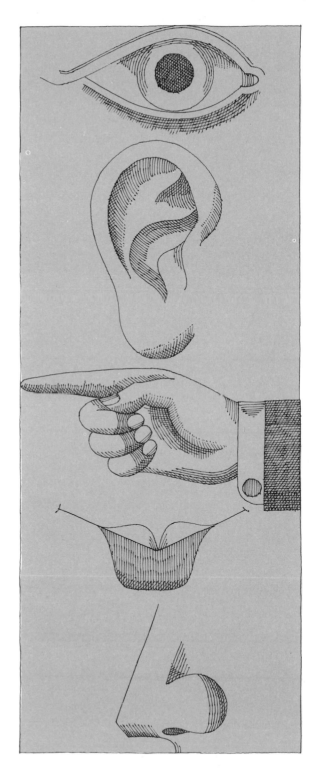

SIX

Tulips, daffodils, and lilies all have Six petals.

Blocks and bricks have Six sides, counting the ends as well, like dice. If you look carefully, you will see that a grain of salt is the same way. So is sugar.

Most cartons of anything except eggs hold Six bottles or cans.

Bugs, like ants and grasshoppers and butterflies and beetles, all have Six legs. That is because they are all insects; anything that does not have Six legs when it has grown up is not an insect. Caterpillars sometimes seem to have lots more than Six legs, but when they grow up and change into butterflies or moths, they have Six legs too.

so that the ones inside are each touching Six others, it looks like a honeycomb. In a honeycomb each cell has Six others right around it.

Christopher Robin was Six years old when he played with Pooh.

"Now I am Six, I'm as clever as clever,
I think I'll be Six for ever and ever."

The Star of David has Six points. You can also see it as two triangles that overlap.

Snowflakes nearly always have Six sides originally, but often they get all thrumbled up with other snowflakes. The best time to see them is when one or two land on a dark colored mitten.

Put a penny on the table and Six others on the table can all touch it at once. If you put a large number of pennies on the table

Six is probably as many times as you can fold a piece of paper in half. Your friends will not believe that.

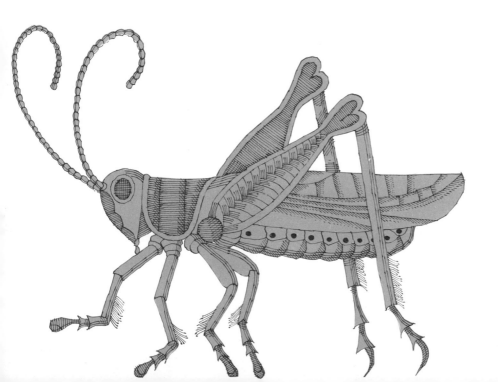

SEVEN

There are Seven days in the week. That's because a long time ago people noticed that there were Seven things in the sky that seemed to move among all the rest. The biggest and brightest is the sun, and so Sunday is the first day of the week. The next is the moon, and Monday is the next day. The names of the rest, except for Saturday, have been altered from the names of the planets that they were originally. Here they are:

Tuesday	Mars' day
Wednesday	Mercury's day
Thursday	Jupiter's day
Friday	Venus' day
Saturday	Saturn's day

There are supposed to be Seven colors in the rainbow: violet, indigo (a kind of dark bluish purple), blue, green, yellow, orange, and red. They don't make good clean stripes,

but are rather smeared into each other. You can remember them by their intials, VIBGYOR, or the other way around, Roy G. Biv.

Also in the sky there is a famous group of stars close together, called the Pleiades. There are Seven of them. The hardest one to see is called Merope, and it is sometimes used to find out how good your eyes are.*

People have always thought that Seven was a lucky number. Most people pick Seven if they are asked to pick a number. A Seventh

* The others are called: Alcyone, Celaeno, Electra, Maia, Sterope, and Taygeta.

son is supposed to be able to do magic; but I have known only two people who could do magic, and neither of them was a Seventh son.

In the same way, at the beach, every Seventh wave is supposed to be larger than the others. Please find out for yourself and tell me if it is true.

The city of Rome was originally built on Seven hills. Not very many people know that Istanbul was also built on Seven hills.

There are Seven deadly sins: greed, sloth, anger, gluttony, envy, pride, and lust.

The brave little tailor in the fairy story

killed Seven flies with one blow of the fly-swatter, and he wrote on his belt: "Seven at a blow."

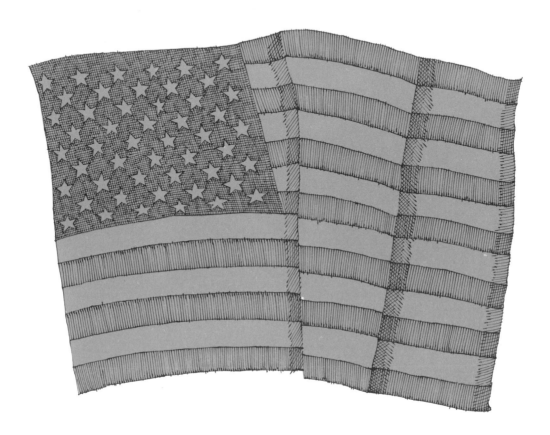

In ancient times, there were Seven Wonders of the World, which were wonderful things built by people, like lighthouses or palaces. Not all versions of them are the same.

There are Seven red stripes in the Stars and Stripes.

EIGHT

Octopuses, spiders, and daddy longlegs all have Eight legs. Nothing with Eight legs has wings (except four birds!).

If you draw Eight squares in a square all touching each other, you get one in the middle free.

A brick has Eight corners.

When they ring bells on a ship to tell sailors the time, they add one more bell every half hour, but Eight is as high as they go. After that they start again.

Most people do not like the number Eight. I do.

The parents of your grandparents are called your great-grandparents. You have Eight of them, though usually most of them have died by now.

them. Some words are several, depending on the way they are used, like:

Well!

Do you think you are well enough to go swimming without an umbrella?

If you push your sister down the well, she will scream.

I am well aware that spanking is too good for you, but it will have to do.

A triolet is a kind of poem and has Eight lines. Most of the well-known triolets are about how difficult they are to write.

A chessboard has Eight squares along each edge, but in China and Japan there is one more.

In most of the world, a stop sign for cars has Eight sides, forming an Octagon.

To play a full scale or an Octave on the piano means to play Eight notes. When you sing them, the notes at both ends are called Do, so that there are not really Eight different names for them.

There are Eight parts of speech, and every word is supposed to be one or another of

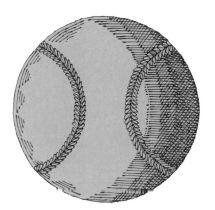

Nine men play on a baseball team.

It takes Nine squares to play tick-tack-toe. Most games of tick-tack-toe end in a draw.

The ancient Greeks made up a frightful monster, called a Hydra. It had Nine heads, each full of sharp teeth. Whenever anybody succeeded in cutting off one of the heads, two more grew in its place; and so I suppose that it ended up with many more than Nine heads before Hercules killed it.

The ancient Greeks also made up Nine Muses, who were spirits who took care of arts and activities, like dancing and plays and music.

A cat-o'-Nine-tails is an old-fashioned whip with lots of ends, not necessarily Nine. It's also a tall kind of plant that grows in swamps.

The pease porridge in the nursery rhyme was Nine days old. Pease porridge is a kind of thick and lumpy pea soup and I don't like it, especially Nine days old, when I should think it would be growing mold.

Nine is often used to mean just a middling large number. So that when we say "A stitch in time saves Nine," we mean that a little trouble early on can save a lot of trouble later. But a Nine days wonder is something or someone that is surprising for just a short time.

Nine months is how long it takes a baby to get ready to be born.

Nine-men's-morris is a game that is not played any more. The idea is to get three men in a row before your opponent. You lay down your men alternately until you each have Nine. Then for each move you slide one of them along the lines. At the Battle of Waterloo the English soldiers played this game in the mud with stones for men.

What does it mean, to say that a cat has Nine lives?

TEN

Ten is a very useful number. Most of the ways of counting invented by men have been based on Ten. This is probably because fingers are very useful for counting.

There are several special words and parts of words in English that have to do with Ten. Most of these words have the letters "dec" in them, which really means Ten.

An army is decimated if every Tenth man is killed.

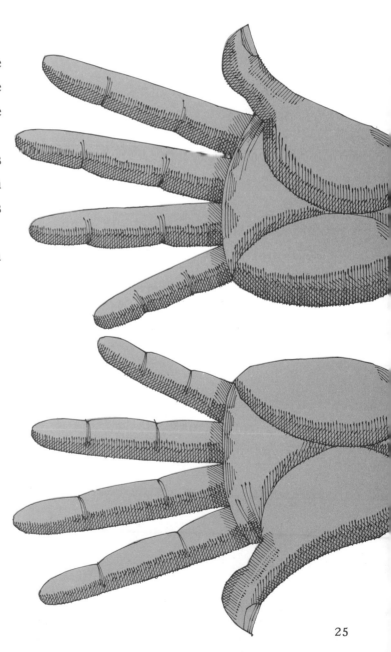

Generally, "deca" means Ten times more, and "deci" means Ten times less. A Deca-dollar is Ten dollars. A Decade is Ten years. A Deci-pizza is one piece of a pizza that has been cut into Ten pieces.

"Pod" means leg in Greek. So that a Deca-

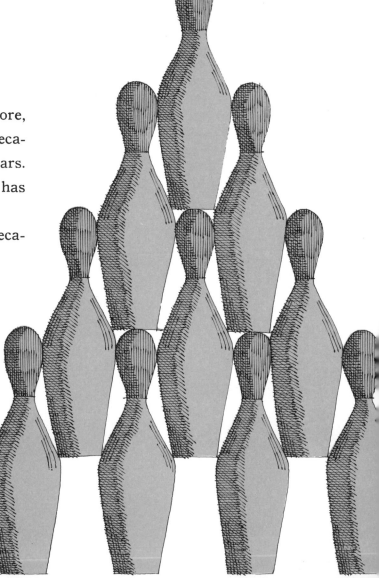

pod is something with Ten legs. Lobsters and squids are Decapods.

In the game of Monopoly, Ten will take you all the way along one edge. If you throw a Ten when you are at Free Parking, you have to Go to Jail (directly, without passing Go, and without collecting $200).

There are Ten pins used in bowling.

Writing the number Ten (10) we start having to use more than one figure. That is very important in arithmetic.

There are Ten teams in each Major League in baseball.

There are Ten Commandments, which Moses found engraved on stone on Mount Sinai, near the north end of the Red Sea.

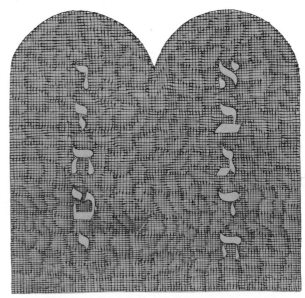

ELEVEN

There are Eleven men playing on a football team, and also Eleven on a cricket team.

To leave something to the Eleventh hour means to leave it until it is nearly too late. Too late would be at midnight, so that the Eleventh hour means Eleven at night, not in the morning.

In England, tea is often served at Eleven o'clock in the morning. When a man is having "his Elevenses," he is having a cup of tea or a snack in the middle of the morning.

I have never found a peapod with more than Eleven peas in it.

Eleven is a quiet number, and I have not been able to find many interesting things that come in Elevens.

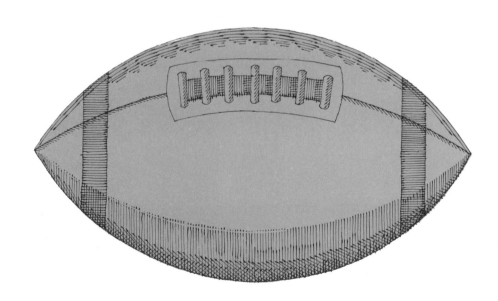

12

TWELVE

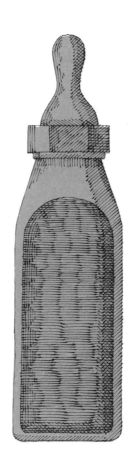

Twelve is another number with special words. Lots of things come in Twelves.

A case of wine or whiskey is Twelve big bottles. It is not really proper to say "My baby brother drank half a case of milk yesterday," because baby bottles are much smaller than wine bottles.

A Dozen of anything is Twelve, except rolls and loaves of bread.* There is even a special word for a Dozen Dozen — Gross. Usually only small things like pencils or paper clips or screws come in Grosses, and not waste baskets or refrigerators.

A carton of eggs is Twelve eggs.

A brick or block has Twelve edges.

Christmas trees are supposed to be decorated and set up shortly before Christmas, and they stay up for the Twelve days of Christmas. On the sixth of January, which is the Feast of the Epiphany, you take them all down.

* See under 13.

Jesus had Twelve Apostles. Their names were: Simon called Peter, Andrew, James son of Zebedee, John, Philip, Bartholomew, Thomas, Matthew, James son of Alpheus, Lebbeus, Simon the Canaanite, and Judas Iscariot.

There are Twelve months in a year, beginning with January and ending with December. December means tenth, because up to a couple of hundred years ago the new year started in March, and December was the tenth month.

There are Twelve main nerves in the head. They all have special names.

There are Twelve inches in a foot, but they don't have special names at all.

In England, Twelve pennies make a shilling.

Clocks work by Twelves, and after Twelve o'clock comes one o'clock, which happens twice a day.

31

13

Thirteen has been thought to be an unlucky number for a long time. This may be because there were thirteen people at the table at the Last Supper before Jesus was crucified. Fear of the number Thirteen has a name — Triskaidekaphobia.

Some big hotels and buildings actually leave the number Thirteen out of their list of floors. And the real Thirteenth is called the fourteenth. The Empire State Building in New York City is one of those.

There are Thirteen cards in each suit of the regulation deck of cards, going from the ace, two, and so on, up to ten, jack, queen, and king. Very often an ace can also rank just above the king, and then the two is the lowest card. Six hundred years ago there was one more card in each suit, another court card, called a chevalier or horseman. (There was also another suit.)

The United States was started by the original Thirteen States; they are New Hampshire, Massachusetts, Rhode Island, Connecticut, New York, New Jersey, Pennsylvania, Delaware, Maryland, Virginia, North Carolina, South Carolina, and Georgia. In honor of them there are Thirteen stripes in the national flag, the Stars and Stripes; the

American eagle holds Thirteen arrows in his left talon and an olive branch with Thirteen leaves in his right one. You can see them quite clearly on a dollar bill.

Juliet was only Thirteen when she fell in love with Romeo and married him.

Traditionally, a baker gives Thirteen rolls or loaves of bread on being asked for a dozen, so that a "baker's dozen" is one more than the usual dozen. Perhaps this is because long ago bakers were not trusted very much and they felt this was a good way to make people think more highly of them.

14
FOURTEEN

There is a special word for Fourteen days or two weeks: a Fortnight. This is obviously a short form of Fourteen-night. It is not used very much in this country, but in England it is more popular.

A sonnet is a kind of short poem, and has Fourteen lines. Shakespeare wrote one hundred fifty-four sonnets.

15
FIFTEEN

If you win Fifteen points at a game of squash, you win the game. Squash is a kind of tennis played indoors, and the small black hard rubber ball bounces off the floor, the walls, and, when I play, off me too.

There were "Fifteen men on a dead man's chest, Yo ho ho and a bottle of rum," in *Treasure Island*. I think it means the other kind of chest.

16

SIXTEEN

U. S. 1375412

In most states, Sixteen is how old you have to be before you can get a driver's license. Sixteen is the middle age of teenagers; there are three teen numbers below Sixteen and three above it.

In the avoirdupois system of weights, a pound has Sixteen ounces for most things; but silver, gold, and platinum are measured in pounds with only twelve ounces, according to the troy system.

20
TWENTY

A Score is a special name for Twenty. Not much these days comes in Scores, and it sounds a little old-fashioned and historical. Most of us know it from the Gettysburg Address, which starts out, "Four score and seven years ago . . ."

There are Twenty cigarettes to the pack.

There are Twenty shillings in a pound in England.

For your Twentieth wedding anniversary you will be given presents made of china, if your friends worry about tradition.

If you manage to live on somebody else's land for Twenty years without his permission, you can usually go on living there even if he wants you to leave.

21
TWENTY-ONE

Twenty-one is a strange number. You have to be Twenty-one to vote almost everywhere, except Georgia, Alaska, Hawaii, and Kentucky.

In table tennis, the winner is the player who first makes Twenty-one points.

The chief unit of money in England is the pound, which is made up of twenty shillings. But Twenty-one shillings is called a guinea, and it is used for telling the price of expensive things like furs, jewelry, and doctors' fees. It is called a guinea because it used to be a coin made from gold from the African country of Guinea.

There is a card game called Twenty-one, which gamblers are very fond of. It is played a lot in places like Nevada and Monte Carlo. Twenty-one is also called Blackjack.

If guns or cannon are fired in salute to important people, Twenty-one is the largest number, and it is only given to presidents and kings. A Twenty-one gun salute is also the salute to the Stars and Stripes.

Legally, people younger than Twenty-one are minors; boys younger than Twenty-one often cannot marry without their parents' permission (but girls only have to be eighteen).

40

FORTY

Forty has often been used to mean a large number, especially in the Bible. It rained Forty days and Forty nights when Noah had built his ark, so that the floods covered all the mountains of the earth. Forty days after he had seen the mountain tops, he sent forth a raven from the ark to see if there was any land to go on. Moses spent Forty days on Mount Sinai and brought back the Ten Commandments. The Israelites and Moses spent Forty years in the wilderness.

If it rains on St. Swithin's day (which is July 15), it is supposed to rain for Forty more days; this rule doesn't seem to work very well.

52

FIFTY-TWO

There are Fifty-two weeks in a year and Fifty-two cards in a deck and Fifty-two white notes on a piano. As far as I know, there is absolutely no connection between these facts.

88

EIGHTY-EIGHT

There are Eighty-eight keys all together on a piano.

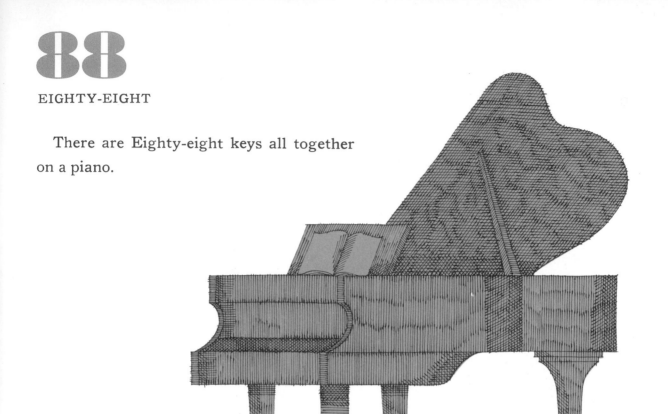

219

TWO HUNDRED NINETEEN

Two dollars and nineteen cents is the largest sum of money in American coins that you can have without being able to make change for anything. You must have a silver dollar, a fifty-cent piece, a quarter, four dimes, and four pennies.

666

SIX HUNDRED SIXTY-SIX

This used to be a famous number — the number of the Devil or the Beast — and anybody who was associated with it was considered to be very bad. In the Middle Ages, a favorite trick to play on an enemy was to show that the letters in his name added up to 666. Of course the letters in his name had to be changed to numbers in some way, such as using the Latin meanings of the letters. My name — oLIVer g. seLfrIDge — adds up to 607, because D = 500, L = 50, V = 5 and I = 1.

1000

ONE THOUSAND

A Thousand is a big number; we might call it the first Very Big Number, or V.B.N. In the Bible it says, "Saul slew his thousands and David his ten thousands." I don't believe that means actually thousands — merely that they had both slain many enemies, but David more than Saul. (That was in the days when killing your enemies was a right and proper thing to do.)

There is a prefix, "kilo-," which means a Thousand of anything. A meter is a little more than a yard and therefore a Kilometer is a little more than a Thousand yards, or more than half a mile. A Kilo-penny is exactly ten dollars. A Kilo-kiss is a kiss every day for nearly three years — that is why a Thousand is a V.B.N.

Another prefix "milli-" means a thousandth part of anything. The paper this is printed on is .... Milli-inches thick, or .... Mills. A Mill also means a Milli-dollar, or a tenth of a cent. A trading stamp is usually worth a Mill. A Milli-Kilo-kiss is just one kiss.

1189

ELEVEN HUNDRED EIGHTY-NINE

Time immemorial is 1189 A.D. This is the only date in this book. Time immemorial is "the time beyond which the memory of man runneth not to the contrary." It is an old legal term.

When I say "I have loved you since time immemorial," it means that I have loved you since 1189 A.D., or for nearly eight hundred years.

63,360

SIXTY-THREE THOUSAND, THREE HUNDRED SIXTY

This is a V.B.N. that is the number of inches in a mile. Your mother is probably a little taller than a milli-mile, or about five feet three and a half inches.

31,536,000

THIRTY-ONE MILLION, FIVE HUNDRED THIRTY-SIX THOUSAND

This V.V.B.N. is the number of seconds in a year. In a leap year there are 31,622,400. The prefix micro-, besides meaning just small, means a millionth part of. "I'll be there in a Micro-year" means to wait about half a minute.

982   F.W.